SINGIN'
IN THE
RAIN

WISE PUBLICATIONS
part of The Music Sales Group
London / New York / Paris / Sydney / Copenhagen / Berlin / Madrid / Hong Kong / Tokyo

SINGIN'
IN THE RAIN

Published by
WISE PUBLICATIONS
14-15 Berners Street, London W1T 3LJ, UK.

Exclusive Distributors:
MUSIC SALES LIMITED
Distribution Centre, Newmarket Road,
Bury St Edmunds, Suffolk IP33 3YB, UK.
MUSIC SALES PTY LIMITED
Units 3-4, 17 Willfox Street, Condell Park,
NSW 2200, Australia.

Order No. AM1006038
ISBN: 978-1-78038-875-5
This book © Copyright 2013 Wise Publications,
a division of Music Sales Limited.

Edited by Jenni Norey.
Music arranged by Derek Jones.
Music processed by Paul Ewers Music Design.
Original design by Dewynters.
Production photography is by Manuel Harlan.
Printed in the EU.

Your Guarantee of Quality:

As publishers, we strive to produce every book
to the highest commercial standards.

This book has been carefully designed to minimise awkward page
turns and to make playing from it a real pleasure.

Particular care has been given to specifying acid-free, neutral-sized paper made
from pulps which have not been elemental chlorine bleached.
This pulp is from farmed sustainable forests and
was produced with special regard for the environment.

Throughout, the printing and binding have been planned to ensure a sturdy,
attractive publication which should give years of enjoyment.

If your copy fails to meet our high standards, please inform us
and we will gladly replace it.

www.musicsales.com

FIT AS A FIDDLE

Words by Arthur Freed
Music by Al Hoffman & Al Goodhart

church bells will be ring-ing and we'll march with ma and pa.____ How the

church bells will be ring-ing with a hey non-ny non-ny and a hot cha cha.____

Hi did-dle did-dle, my ba-by's O. K.____ Ask me a rid-dle and what does she say?____

Fit as a fid-dle and read-y for love.

YOU STEPPED OUT OF A DREAM

Words by Gus Kahn
Music by Nacio Herb Brown

Song And Dance Man

Music by Dave Mann & Bob Hilliard

ALL I DO IS DREAM OF YOU

Words by Arthur Freed
Music by Nacio Herb Brown

ev - 'ry throught, you're ev - 'ry-thing, you're ev - 'ry song I ev - er sing.

Sum - mer, win - ter, au - tumn and spring. And

were there more than twen - ty four hours a day

may - be spent in sweet con - tent, dream - ing a - way. When

13

skies are grey, when skies are blue, morn-ing, noon and night-time too,___

all I do the whole day through is dream of you.___

You're the cat's me - ow!

All I do the whole day through is dream of you.

MAKE 'EM LAUGH

Words by Arthur Freed
Music by Nacio Herb Brown

BEAUTIFUL GIRL

Words by Arthur Freed & Reginald Connelly
Music by Nacio Brown

YOU ARE MY LUCKY STAR

Words by Arthur Freed
Music by Nacio Herb Brown

Spoken: *Lucky?* *I wonder.* *I wonder how many girls would consider it lucky...*

You're my Fair - banks, my Mo - re - no. Rod La Rocque and

Va - len - ti - no. You are my

luck - y star.

YOU WERE MEANT FOR ME

Words by Arthur Freed
Music by Nacio Herb Brown

meant you just for me.

But I'm con - tent the an - gels must have sent you, and they meant you just for me.

MOSES SUPPOSES

Words by Betty Comden & Adolph Green
Music by Roger Edens

Mos-es sup-pos-es his toes-es are ros-es but Mos-es sup-pos-es er-ro-ne-ous-ly.___ But

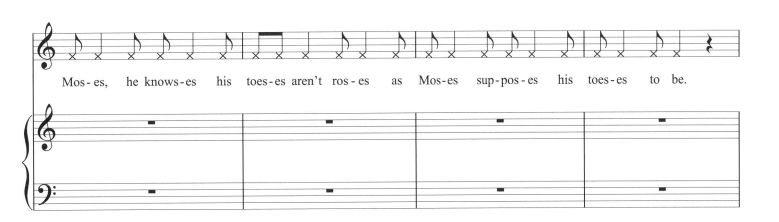

Mos-es, he knows-es his toes-es aren't ros-es as Mos-es sup-pos-es his toes-es to be.

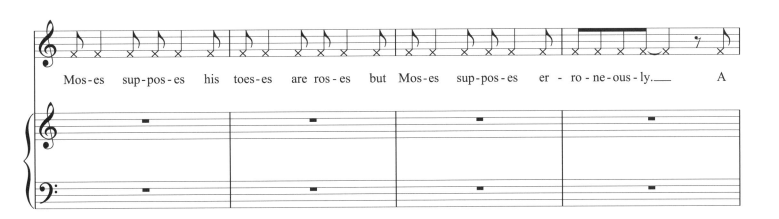

Mos-es sup-pos-es his toes-es are ros-es but Mos-es sup-pos-es er-ro-ne-ous-ly.___ A

GOOD MORNING

Words by Arthur Freed
Music by Nacio Herb Brown

morn - in', good morn - in',___ it's great to stay up late.___ Good

morn - in', good morn - in' to you.

When the band___ be - gan___ to play___ the stars___ were shin - ing bright.___

___ Now the milk - man's on his way,___ it's too

42

SINGIN' IN THE RAIN

Words by Arthur Freed
Music by Nacio Herb Brown

Danc - in' in the rain.   Da de da_____ da dya de dya.

I'm hap - py a - gain.

I'm

sing - in'_____ and danc - in'   in   the   rain.

48

I'm danc-in'_____ and sing-in' in the rain.

49

WOULD YOU?

Words by Arthur Freed
Music by Nacio Herb Brown

met as you and I and they were on - ly friends.

But be - fore the sto - ry ends, he'll

a tempo

kiss her with a sigh, would you? Would you? And

if the girl were I, would you? Would you? And

WHAT'S WRONG WITH ME?

Words by Edward Heyman
Music by Nacio Herb Brown

BROADWAY MELODY

Words by Arthur Freed
Music by Nacio Herb Brown

BROADWAY RHYTHM

Words by Arthur Freed
Music by Nacio Herb Brown

Broad - way____ rhy - thm,____ it's got____ me, ev - 'ry - bod - y

dance!_____

Broad - way____ rhy - thm,____ it's got____ me, ev - 'ry - bod - y

sing   and   dance!

Oh,_____ that Broad - way

rhy - thm.